April 14, 1970, p.m.

Apollo 13 makes its closest approach to the Moon, having called off the planned lunar landing.

1995

A dramatic film of the mission starring Tom Hanks is released, renewing people's interest in this historic event.

April 17, 1970

A plan is put into action to return the crew to Earth. The command module is powered up from shutdown. The crew manages to land the craft successfully back on Earth and is rescued.

Space travel—where next?

The Moon is Earth's only natural satellite. It orbits our planet at a distance of around 384,400 kilometres (238,855 miles), and takes about 27 Earth days to complete a single orbit.

In comparison, Venus, the closest planet to Earth, is 41,400,000 km (25,724,767 miles) away! No manned mission to Venus has ever been planned, since this planet has an extremely hot and inhospitable atmosphere.

Mars, however, is being considered as the next destination for human space exploration. Mars is 78,340,000 km (48,678,219 miles) from Earth, and it may take between 7 and 10 months of travelling through space for us to reach it. There is also no guarantee that the astronauts would return!

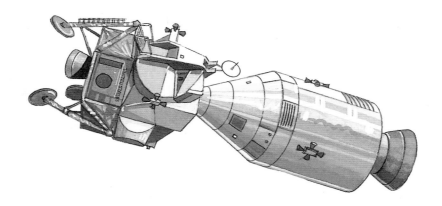

Author:

Ian Graham was born in Belfast in 1953.
He studied applied physics at City University,
London, where he later earned a postgraduate
degree in journalism, specialising in science
and technology. He has written more than one
hundred children's nonfiction books and numerous
magazine articles.

Artist:

David Antram was born in Brighton, England,
in 1958. He studied at Eastbourne College of Art
and then worked in advertising for 15 years before
becoming a full-time artist. He has illustrated
many children's nonfiction books.

Series Creator:

David Salariya was born in Dundee, Scotland.
He has illustrated a wide range of books and has
created and designed many new series for
publishers both in the U.K. and overseas. In 1989,
he established The Salariya Book Company.
He lives in Brighton, England, with his wife,
illustrator Shirley Willis, and their son, Jonathan.

Editor:

Karen Barker Smith

Published in Great Britain in MMXIX by
Book House, an imprint of
The Salariya Book Company Ltd
25 Marlborough Place, Brighton BN1 1UB
www.salariya.com

ISBN: 978-1-912537-30-3

SCRIBO   BOOK HOUSE   SCRIBBLERS

1 3 5 7 9 8 6 4 2

A CIP catalogue record for this book is available
from the British Library.
Printed and bound in China.

Visit
www.salariya.com
for our online catalogue and
free fun stuff.

PAPER FROM

SUSTAINABLE
FORESTS

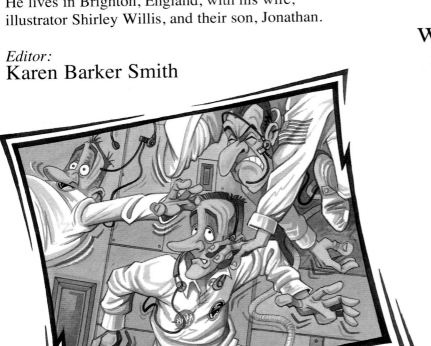

You Wouldn't Want to Be™ on Apollo 13!

I'm sure 13 is an unlucky number!

A Mission You'd Rather Not Go On

Written by
Ian Graham

Illustrated by
David Antram

Created and designed by
David Salariya

BOOK HOUSE
a SALARIYA imprint

Contents

Introduction

It is April 1970. You are an American astronaut about to climb into a spacecraft and fly to the Moon. You have been training for years for the chance to take part in this mission. You watched two members of the Apollo 11 crew, Neil Armstrong and Buzz Aldrin, become the first people ever to walk on another world. They landed on the Moon in July 1969. They were followed by Charles Conrad and Alan Bean of the Apollo 12 mission in November that year. The whole world watched them explore the Moon on television.

Now it is your turn. You are a member of the three-man crew of Apollo 13. Some people think that 13 is an unlucky number – you don't know it yet, but Apollo 13 will be an incredibly unlucky mission. On your way to the Moon, your spacecraft will suffer the most serious accident to happen during a Moon-landing mission. It is so serious that no one knows if you will be able to get back to Earth. Your fate depends on hundreds of engineers on Earth working out how to get you home safely. You wouldn't want to be on Apollo 13!

Practise makes perfect

The whole crew practises everything that you will have to do during the mission. You do it over and over again until you could do it in your sleep. You train in simulators that look exactly like the real spacecraft. The mission controllers keep you on your toes by surprising you with all sorts of emergencies to see how well you deal with them. If you're going to make a mistake, it is better to do it in the simulator than on the way to the Moon. By the time launch day comes, you have to know the spacecraft inside out, be able to fly it perfectly and know what to do in any situation.

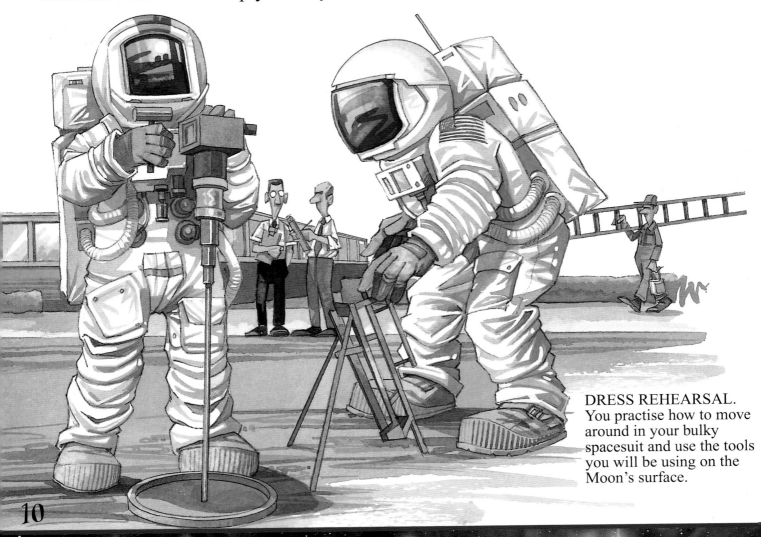

DRESS REHEARSAL. You practise how to move around in your bulky spacesuit and use the tools you will be using on the Moon's surface.

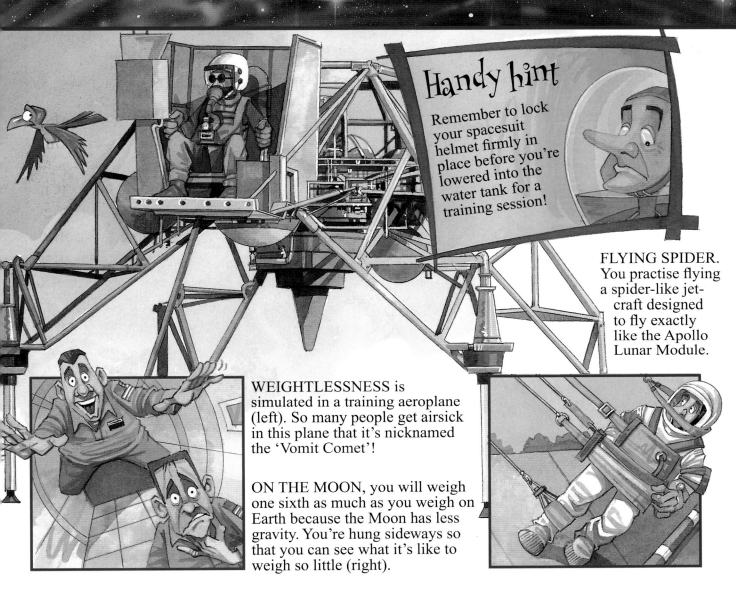

Handy hint

Remember to lock your spacesuit helmet firmly in place before you're lowered into the water tank for a training session!

FLYING SPIDER. You practise flying a spider-like jet-craft designed to fly exactly like the Apollo Lunar Module.

WEIGHTLESSNESS is simulated in a training aeroplane (left). So many people get airsick in this plane that it's nicknamed the 'Vomit Comet'!

ON THE MOON, you will weigh one sixth as much as you weigh on Earth because the Moon has less gravity. You're hung sideways so that you can see what it's like to weigh so little (right).

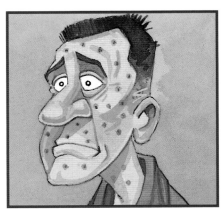

UNDERWATER. You practise making spacewalks in a huge water tank (left). The uplift you get from the water provides the closest thing to weightlessness on Earth.

BUG ALERT! Someone the crew works with catches German measles. To avoid becoming ill in space, one crew member with no immunity to it is replaced two days before launch.

11

The Apollo spacecraft

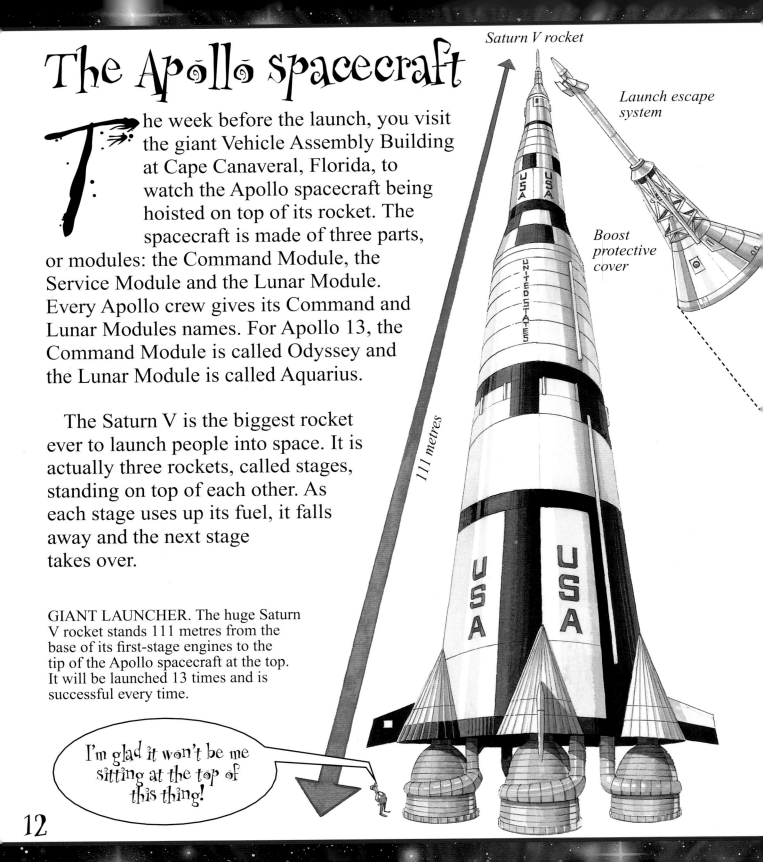

The week before the launch, you visit the giant Vehicle Assembly Building at Cape Canaveral, Florida, to watch the Apollo spacecraft being hoisted on top of its rocket. The spacecraft is made of three parts, or modules: the Command Module, the Service Module and the Lunar Module. Every Apollo crew gives its Command and Lunar Modules names. For Apollo 13, the Command Module is called Odyssey and the Lunar Module is called Aquarius.

The Saturn V is the biggest rocket ever to launch people into space. It is actually three rockets, called stages, standing on top of each other. As each stage uses up its fuel, it falls away and the next stage takes over.

GIANT LAUNCHER. The huge Saturn V rocket stands 111 metres from the base of its first-stage engines to the tip of the Apollo spacecraft at the top. It will be launched 13 times and is successful every time.

Saturn V rocket

Launch escape system

Boost protective cover

111 metres

I'm glad it won't be me sitting at the top of this thing!

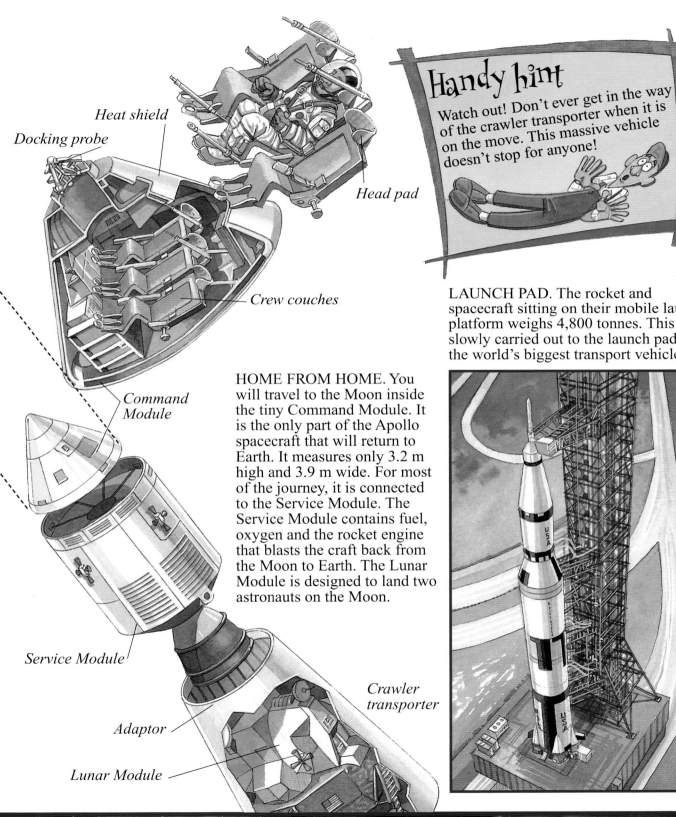

Heat shield

Docking probe

Head pad

Crew couches

Command Module

Service Module

Adaptor

Lunar Module

Crawler transporter

LAUNCH PAD. The rocket and spacecraft sitting on their mobile launch platform weighs 4,800 tonnes. This is slowly carried out to the launch pad by the world's biggest transport vehicle.

HOME FROM HOME. You will travel to the Moon inside the tiny Command Module. It is the only part of the Apollo spacecraft that will return to Earth. It measures only 3.2 m high and 3.9 m wide. For most of the journey, it is connected to the Service Module. The Service Module contains fuel, oxygen and the rocket engine that blasts the craft back from the Moon to Earth. The Lunar Module is designed to land two astronauts on the Moon.

13

Launch day
Countdown to takeoff

WAKEY, WAKEY! You are called precisely four hours and 17 minutes before launch.

SAY 99. The flight doctor gives you a final once-over four hours and two minutes before launch to make sure you are in top condition.

aunch day has arrived. It is 11th April 1970. Your 400,000-kilometre journey to the Moon begins a few hours from now with a trip into orbit around the Earth. While you and the rest of the crew go through your preparations for takeoff, a team of engineers gets the spacecraft and its mighty rocket ready for you. You can't waste any time. Everything, from filling the rocket's fuel tanks to having your breakfast, has its own time slot in the carefully planned countdown. It's too late to change your mind now!

BREAKFAST. At 'eggs-actly' three hours and 32 minutes before launch, you have breakfast – steak, eggs, orange juice, coffee and toast – and then put on your spacesuit.

SNOOPY CAP. This soft cap (4) contains earpieces and a microphone for radio communications. A clear 'fishbowl' helmet (5) locks onto the top of the suit and gloves lock onto metal rings at the ends of the sleeves (6).

SUITING UP. The various parts of the spacesuit are put on in order. Electrodes (1) are glued to your chest to monitor your heartbeat. Underwear – a pair of 'long johns' (2) – is the first layer next to the skin. Next, you pull on the spacesuit legs, push your head through the neck ring and pull on the body and arms (3).

14

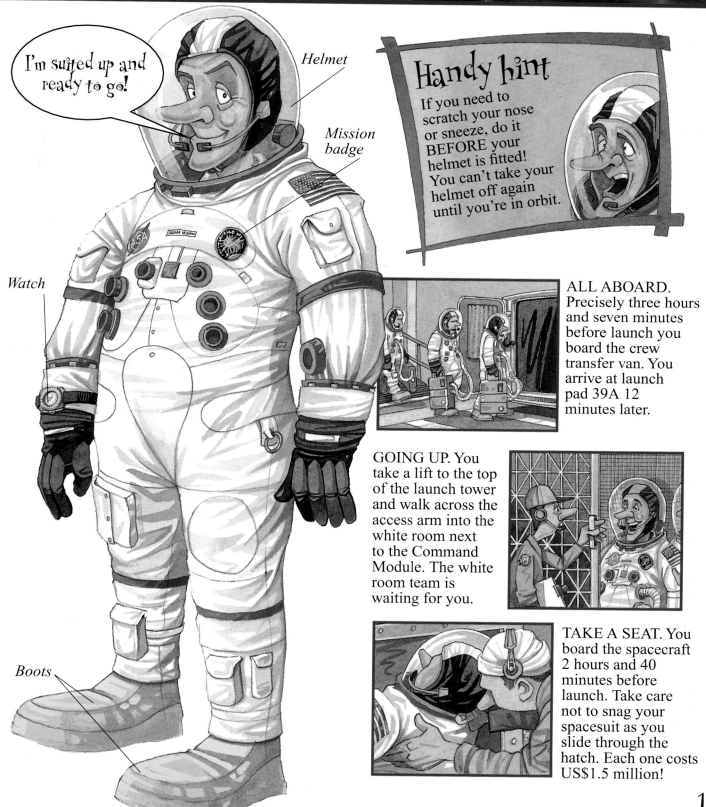

I'm suited up and ready to go!

Helmet

Mission badge

Watch

Boots

Handy hint
If you need to scratch your nose or sneeze, do it BEFORE your helmet is fitted! You can't take your helmet off again until you're in orbit.

ALL ABOARD. Precisely three hours and seven minutes before launch you board the crew transfer van. You arrive at launch pad 39A 12 minutes later.

GOING UP. You take a lift to the top of the launch tower and walk across the access arm into the white room next to the Command Module. The white room team is waiting for you.

TAKE A SEAT. You board the spacecraft 2 hours and 40 minutes before launch. Take care not to snag your spacesuit as you slide through the hatch. Each one costs US$1.5 million!

Liftoff!

When the countdown reaches zero, you start a 12-minute rollercoaster ride through Earth's atmosphere to space. As the rocket leaves the launch pad, the time on the clock at Mission Control in Houston, Texas, is 13.13! Pictures of the soaring rocket and its flight path appear on a big display screen at Mission Control.

T (TAKEOFF) –3 MINUTES, 7 SECONDS. The Saturn V rocket is given the firing command that starts its automatic launch sequence. Computers start its fuel pumps.

T –8.9 SECONDS. The first-stage engines fire. The rocket is held down on the launch pad until all five engines are running.

ZERO. Apollo 13 and the 3,000-tonne Saturn V launch-rocket gently lift off the launch pad.

RROOARR

16

Apollo 13's bad luck first strikes when one of the rocket engines shuts down two minutes early. For a few moments, you don't know if Apollo 13 will make it into space. The remaining engines fire for longer to make up for the fault. Engineers at Mission Control check that there is enough fuel left to send the spacecraft to the Moon.

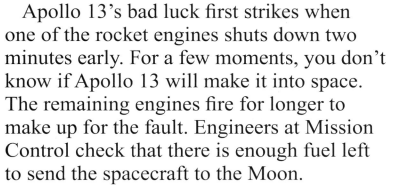

Handy hint

Crash

Bounce

Make sure you are strapped tightly into your seat. If you aren't, you'll bounce around the Command Module like a cork in a bottle when the rocket blasts off!

T +3 MINUTES, 20 SECONDS. The launch escape tower's rockets fire, carrying the tower and boost protective cover away from the top of the spacecraft.

T +2 MINUTES, 44 SECONDS. The empty first stage falls away and 2 seconds later the second-stage engines fire.

T +9 MINUTES, 53 SECONDS. The empty second stage falls away. Three seconds later, the third-stage engines fire.

T +12 MINUTES, 39 SECONDS. The spacecraft is safely in orbit around Earth. Time to check that everything is working properly.

17

Goodbye Earth

The spacecraft checks out fine, so you get the go-ahead to fire the third-stage engine and head for the Moon. The engine boosts your speed from 28,000 kilometres per hour (kph) to the 40,000 kph needed to break away from Earth's gravity. Once you are safely on your way to the Moon, there is a very important job to do. The Lunar Module is packed away inside the top of the rocket, underneath the Command and Service Modules (CSM). The CSM has to be separated from the rocket and turned around so that it can pull the Lunar Module out. This delicate manoeuvre requires pinpoint flying. Nothing less will do.

STEADY AS YOU GO. Thrusters nudge the spacecraft slowly forwards and away from the end of Saturn V's third stage (above).

TURNAROUND. The thrusters are fired again to turn the spacecraft around. The end of the rocket opens up like a giant flower, revealing the Lunar Module (above).

STEERING. You steer the spacecraft by using hand controllers to fire rocket thrusters on the Service Module.

Piece of cake!

Handy hint

If you suffer from space sickness, grab a bag fast. Remember, during weightlessness EVERYTHING floats around the spacecraft – yuck!

Docking probe

DOCKING. The CSM eases forwards and docks with the Lunar Module (above). A probe on top of it fits into a hole on top of the Lunar Module and the two craft lock together.

EASY DOES IT. The CSM slowly backs up and pulls the Lunar Module out of the end of the rocket (above). It all goes perfectly. You are on your way.

19

Living in a tin can

Being an Apollo astronaut sometimes feels like living inside a tiny tin can. You have to get along with two other people in that small space for more than a week. You have to get used to noise all the time too. The spacecraft is never completely silent. There is the hum of air pumps, voices on the radio and the sounds of other crew-members moving about. The temperature is kept at a steady 22°C, so once you're in orbit, you can take off the bulky spacesuit you wore for the launch and put on a more comfortable flight suit. In orbit you experience weightlessness and can just float around inside the spacecraft.

SPACE FOOD. You wish you could eat 'normal' food. Most space food is dried to save weight in the spacecraft (left). You add water to make it edible.

GOING TO THE TOILET. Three astronauts produce a lot of urine during a mission. To save weight, it is dumped overboard (right).

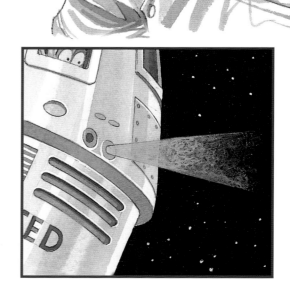

Handy hint

There is no 'up' or 'down' in space. You can work just as easily standing on your head as with your feet on the floor.

Be careful where you're floating!

THE BARBECUE ROLL. The spacecraft spins constantly, very slowly, so that it is heated evenly by the Sun (left).

TV STAR. You present television reports, or telecasts, from the spacecraft to show viewers how the flight is going (right).

21

Houston, we've had a problem

n 13th April, Apollo 13 is 329,000 km away from Earth. Each day the Moon looks bigger through the Command Module windows. Mission Control asks you to turn on fans inside the Service Module's oxygen tanks. As soon as the switch is hit, you hear a loud bang. You watch your instruments in horror. The spacecraft seems to be losing oxygen and electrical power. You struggle to understand what has happened. Mission controllers on Earth can't believe what they see on their computer screens.

Disaster strikes

1. THE JOLT. You hear a bang and the spacecraft shakes violently. You think it might have been hit by a piece of space rock.

2. ALARMS go off in the spacecraft and at Mission Control. You watch your instruments in disbelief.

Handy hint

Don't panic! If something goes wrong, it's important to keep calm or you might make things even worse.

3. WHAT'S HAPPENING? Mission controllers think their computers have gone crazy. Their screens don't seem to make sense.

4. GAS ESCAPE. You look through a window and see something spraying out into space. It must be oxygen!

5. LOSING POWER. Your instruments show that the Command Module's fuel cells are losing power fast.

6. MOVE OUT! You quickly power down the Command Module and move into the Lunar Module so that you can use its air and electricity.

BANG!!

WHAT HAPPENED? Later, it is discovered that an electrical fault blew up an oxygen tank and damaged equipment in the Service Module.

23

Failure is not an option

At Mission Control, the flight director tells everyone to find a way to get the crew home. He shouts, 'Failure is not an option!' Ground controllers and engineers immediately start discussing what to do. Some of them want to turn the spacecraft around and bring it straight back to Earth. Others want to let the spacecraft keep going and use the Moon's gravity to swing it round and back to Earth. This option would take longer. The long way would be less risky, but no one knows if the spacecraft's oxygen and electricity will last long enough. You keep calling Mission Control to ask for their decision, but they're still working out what to do for the best.

Option one

The spacecraft does a U-turn and comes straight home. It gets you home fast, but you would have to fire the Service Module engine. It might be damaged, it might not work and it might explode.

Handy hint

Watch your instruments like a hawk. They tell you exactly what is happening in the rest of the spacecraft, especially all the parts that you can't see.

Those are our options, gentlemen. Let's get those astronauts home safely.

Option two

Mission controllers decide it's safer to carry on to the Moon and swing behind it. You can use the Lunar Module engine to stay on course, but it wasn't designed for this. Will this plan work?

Cold, wet and stuffy

Keeping warm is not as important as getting home alive, so the spacecraft heaters are switched off to save electricity. The temperature falls to just above freezing. Moisture from your breath condenses on the cold instrument panels, walls and windows. The whole spacecraft is wet. It is dark too, because most of the lights are switched off. It gets very stuffy – the Lunar Module was designed for two astronauts, not three, so it can't purify the air fast enough. The breathed-out carbon dioxide in the air rises to a dangerous level. If it continues to rise, you will lose consciousness! You have to do something about it.

A wee problem!

The crippled spacecraft is so hard to control that you have to stop dumping urine overboard. When it sprays out into space it pushes the spacecraft off course. So you have to save it all in plastic bags and store them inside the spacecraft!

A bit of do-it-yourself

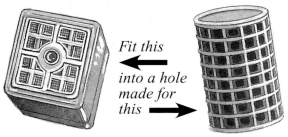

Fit this into a hole made for this ← →

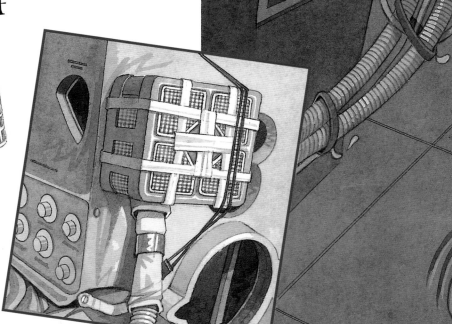

The Command Module has air purifier canisters that could freshen the air, but they are square. The fittings in the Lunar Module are round. You make them fit by using pieces of hose, sticky tape, plastic bags and rubber bands (right). It works! The amount of carbon dioxide in the air starts falling.

Lost mission

If everything had gone as planned, Apollo 13 would have landed on part of the Moon called Fra Mauro. Apollo 11 and 12 landed in the Sea of Tranquillity and the Ocean of Storms. The ground there was flat because lava had flowed over it. Scientists wanted samples of older rocks from the hills and mountains that hadn't been covered by lava, but these places are more dangerous to land. The earlier missions proved that astronauts could fly the Lunar Module manually and choose a safe landing spot. It was decided that Aquarius from Apollo 13 would land in the Fra Mauro hills.

SPACESUIT. The spacesuit you would have worn on the Moon (right) has extra-tough gloves, boots and a visor over the helmet to keep your head cool. You would also have worn a backpack with oxygen and a radio.

If nothing had gone wrong...

MOON ROCKS. You would have collected lots of Moon rocks and brought them back to Earth.

HEAT FLOW. You would have drilled holes in the Moon's surface to test how heat flows through it.

What a fantastic view!

Handy hint

Be careful not to fall over on your back or you could be stranded there. You would not be able to get up because of the Moon's low gravity.

SOLAR WIND. You would have collected samples of the solar wind – particles that stream out of the Sun and hit the Moon.

PHOTOGRAPHY. You would have taken thousands of close-up photographs of dust, rocks and craters on the Moon's surface.

MOONQUAKES. You were planning to put instruments on the Moon's surface to detect the vibrations of moonquakes.

LONE ORBITER. While two astronauts explored the surface, the third would orbit the Moon alone in the Command Module.

Going home

Y ou receive new instructions from Mission Control. You are to fire the Lunar Module's descent stage engine to change course. If it works it will send you around the Moon and back to Earth. This engine was not designed to be used like this. It is the engine that would have slowed the Lunar Module down as it approached the Moon's surface. The engine has to be fired before you reach the Moon and again just after you reappear from behind it. While you are behind the Moon, you are out of contact with Mission Control. If something goes wrong, no one can help you.

Lunar Module

Command and Service Module (CSM)

NERVOUS WAIT. As the spacecraft disappears behind the Moon, everyone in Mission Control can only wait and hope that the burn (the firing of the engine) has gone well.

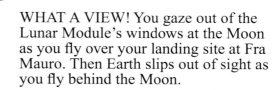

WHAT A VIEW! You gaze out of the Lunar Module's windows at the Moon as you fly over your landing site at Fra Mauro. Then Earth slips out of sight as you fly behind the Moon.

Handy hint

Remember to close the Command Module hatch before you undock the Lunar Module and cast it adrift. Otherwise you'll be sucked out into space!

That would've been a great place to visit.

BURN 1. The Lunar Module engine fires perfectly for 35 seconds, speeding you on your way behind the Moon.

FIRST SIGHT. When the Service Module is finally cast adrift, you gasp as you catch your first sight of the damage (left). The explosion has blown out one whole side, from top to bottom.

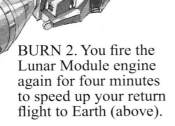

BURN 2. You fire the Lunar Module engine again for four minutes to speed up your return flight to Earth (above).

GOODBYE LUNAR MODULE. You power up the damp, cold and dark Command Module and prepare for your return to Earth. You cast the Lunar Module adrift (right) and say goodbye to the craft that acted as your lifeboat.

31

Down to Earth

You are nearly home but you still face the most dangerous part of the mission – re-entering the Earth's atmosphere. It is very important to keep the spacecraft on course so that it hits the atmosphere at the right angle. If it comes in at the wrong angle it will either burn up or bounce off.

The heat shield glows red hot. It is all that stands between you and the extreme heat outside. No one knows if it was damaged by the explosion. The air around the spacecraft gets so hot that radio waves can't get through. You can't talk to Mission Control and they can't hear you. They do not know if you are alive or dead.

TOO SHALLOW. A spacecraft hitting Earth's atmosphere at too shallow an angle would bounce off it like a stone skipping across water.

TOO STEEP. If the Command Module dives into the atmosphere at too steep an angle, it will get too hot and burn up.

CHUTES OPEN. The Command Module falls through the clouds and floats down under three huge parachutes.

Handy hint

When you step out onto the deck of the recovery ship don't get too close to anyone — remember, you haven't had a bath for a whole week!

WELCOME HOME. You step out of the helicopter onto the deck of the recovery ship and wave to the crew and cameras.

'13 CALLING'. Cheering breaks out at Mission Control as the radio crackles into life and you report in (above).

SPLASHDOWN. The module hits the ocean with a mighty splash (below left). You're safely back on Earth.

Divers knock on the spacecraft hatch (below) and help you out to a waiting helicopter.

33

Glossary

Boost protective cover The cover that protected the Apollo Command Module during launch.

Burn A short firing of a rocket engine to change a spacecraft's course.

Canisters A container, usually made of metal.

Cape Canaveral A place in Florida, USA, where the John F. Kennedy Space Center is located. Many space flights are launched from there.

Carbon dioxide A gas that is breathed out by people.

Command Module The cone-shaped part of an Apollo spacecraft where the crew lived.

Crawler transporter The giant vehicle that moved Saturn V rockets from their assembly building to the launch pad.

CSM The Command and Service Module, a spacecraft made from the Command Module and Service Module linked together.

Fuel cell A device that uses oxygen and hydrogen gases to make electricity and water.

Gravity The force that pulls everything towards a large object such as a planet or moon.

Hatch A doorway in a spacecraft.

Heat shield The part of a spacecraft that protects the rest of the craft from the heat of re-entry.

Launch escape tower A rocket designed to fly the Command Module away to safety in an emergency during launch.

Lava Molten rock that flows out onto the surface of a planet or moon.

Lunar Module The part of an Apollo spacecraft designed to land on the Moon.

Manually Done by hand instead of being done automatically by machines.

Mission Control The building where the space flights are monitored and managed.

Orbit To travel in a circle around a planet or moon.

Oxygen A gas humans need to breathe. It was also used to make water and electricity in the Apollo spacecraft.

Particle An extremely small piece or speck of something.

Recovery ship A ship sent to where a spacecraft is expected to land to pick up the crew.

Re-entry Coming back into the Earth's atmosphere from space.

Service Module The part of an Apollo spacecraft that supplied the Command Module with oxygen, water, electricity and rocket power.

Simulator A machine made to look like a vehicle, such as a spacecraft, used to train pilots.

Stage Part of a larger rocket with its own engine or engines, that falls away when its fuel is used up.

Thruster A small rocket engine used to adjust the position of a spacecraft while in space.

Index

The Moon

For centuries, stargazers have marvelled at the Moon in the sky. To the ancient Egyptians, the Moon was the symbol of Thoth, the god of wisdom. Throughout history, people looking at the craters on the Moon's surface have been reminded of the shapes of animals or a giant human face.

Hundreds of years before astronauts set foot on the Moon, people were already dreaming of travelling through space. In the 16th century, English author Francis Godwin wrote a story about a trip to the Moon. In it, the hero is towed to the Moon by a team of wild swans.

In 1865, French author Jules Verne wrote a science-fiction book called *From the Earth to the Moon*, about a club of weapons enthusiasts in post-Civil War America who build an enormous cannon and blast themselves to the Moon in a projectile.

Although Jules Verne's book leaves the fate of these brave voyagers unclear, English author H.G. Wells's later story *The First Men in the Moon* is more detailed. It tells the story of a businessman and an eccentric scientist who fly to the Moon in a spaceship, where they discover a superintelligent civilisation of insect-like creatures living beneath its surface. These fantastical tales inspired later scientists to come up with ways of reaching the Moon for real.

Top Events in the Space Race

Rockets

By the early 20th century a Russian inventor, Konstantin Tsiolkovsky, thought of using rockets to reach space. In 1903 he suggested that liquid fuel should be used to power rockets, since it could be controlled more easily.

V-2

During World War II, Wernher von Braun developed a rocket-powered missile in Germany called the V-2. After the war, von Braun lived in the United States, where he went on to mastermind the American space programme, including the Apollo launches.

The Cold War

This was a time of hostility between the Soviet Union and the United States that began after World War II. Both nations wanted to prove that their scientists were making great technological advances.

The Americans believed that their technology was superior, until the Soviets shot a satellite, Sputnik 1, into space in 1957.

Yuri Gagarin

On April 12, 1961, the Soviets put the first man in space. Major Yuri Gagarin was the first cosmonaut – the Russian word for astronaut. He made a single orbit of Earth in his Vostok spacecraft, and became a worldwide celebrity.

NASA

Gagarin's success embarrassed the United States. America's National Aeronautics and Space Administration (NASA) had been formed in 1958; its aim was to put a man in space. In May 1961, the new president, John F. Kennedy, vowed that the United States would place a man on the Moon and return him safely to Earth before 1970.

Did You Know?

On July 20, 1969, Apollo 11 was the first manned mission to land on the Moon. The crew was flight commander Neil Armstrong, lunar module pilot Buzz Aldrin and the command module pilot Michael Collins.

Neil Armstrong was the first man to walk on the Moon. 'That's one small step for a man, one giant leap for mankind,' he said, as he stepped onto the Moon. His words became one of the most famous quotes of all time.

There have been six manned Moon landings by U.S. spacecraft, which were carried out between 1969 and 1972. In total, 18 astronauts travelled to the Moon during these missions.

In recent years, the space above Earth has become very crowded with satellites and space junk (pieces of broken old rockets and worn-out satellites). There is a serious danger of collisions.

There are close to 100 bags of poo on the Moon, left there over the years by astronauts of Apollo missions. The lack of wind and rain mean they're still perfectly preserved.